Approaches to
Spiritual Direction

Anne Long

Canon Emeritus, Guildford Cathedral

Now Retired in Salisbury

GROVE BOOKS LIMITED
RIDLEY HALL RD CAMBRIDGE CB3 9HU

Contents

The Cover Illustration is by Graham Pigott

First Impression May 1984
Second Edition (by Grove Books Ltd) February 1988
Third Edition July 1998
Fourth Edition February 2005
ISSN 0262-799X
ISBN 1 85174 072 4

Introduction

1

Some readers may get no further than the title of this book suggesting, as it seems to, something austere, authoritarian, Catholic and far removed from their own experience!

But for those who open it, let me say what it is about.

Firstly, I hope to clarify what spiritual direction is—and what it is not—for it represents a tremendously rich tradition in the church's history which, by its very nature, has been both a hidden and profound influence in the lives of many. Some will have associated direction with Catholic rather than evangelical tradition and for that reason will not know much about it. If this booklet does no more than whet your appetite, the bibliography will take you further.

Secondly, I hope to encourage readers to consider spiritual direction as a personal resource, whether in the traditional one-to-one way or in the context of a support group. All of us—leaders and lay people—need regular opportunity for stock-taking and replenishment if we are to minister effectively. A clergyman in his late thirties recently said: 'No-one has asked me about my praying since I was ordained!'—whether he wanted anyone to ask him was not clear, but the implication was that he needed it! Our clerical structures do not necessarily make it easy for pastors to be pastored. Simon Barrington-Ward wrote 'We certainly have an experience all over the world of church leaders in loneliness needing to submit themselves to others, and this is a crying need that is just not being met.' But spiritual direction can also provide a resource for lay people wanting to grow in Christian discipleship. I hope to encourage some to seek and find.

One of my excitements has been to learn about prayer and discipleship from Christians of other traditions. It was in the context of 'direction' that I first met Julian of Norwich and subsequently a wealth of other spiritual classics. An Anglo-Catholic priest helped me accept the desert experiences of prayer—no-one had ever told me, after an experience of personal renewal, to expect the stripping and refining that was not a falling from grace but a growth in it. It was through 'direction' from an Anglican monk that I learnt more about spiritual warfare and the mysteries of pain in intercession. For all his enclosure he seemed remarkably in touch with the world. More recently, at a Roman Catholic retreat, where we were asked to use no book other than the Bible, the personal daily direction given became a memorable means of the Holy Spirit's teaching, healing, and guiding. A 'cell' group of colleagues in my days at St John's College also proved an important means of personal review and direction for me and other colleagues. I mention these examples thankfully—they are all to do with spiritual direction and have brought learning that I might never have received within one tradition alone.

Thirdly, I hope to indicate ways in which spiritual direction might be developed as a means of nurture within the church. As Christians are taught so they must be enabled to teach others also. And this need not be just the prerogative (and burden) of leaders but develop into a healthy mutuality between lay people, as is already happening in various parts of the church.

2　The Search for Direction

1 In Society

A wide variety of experience and direction is on offer. Throughout the '60s and '70s there was an upsurge of movements and groups aiming to raise the level of consciousness and to offer religious and spiritual experience to those seeking personal meaning and direction. And to guide people there was (and is) no lack of gurus, exotic and otherwise. Some psychologists are now investigating, with greater interest than previously, phenomenological and transpersonal experience. Carl Rogers, after 45 years as a humanist clinical psychologist, has challenged fellow psychologists to consider 'the possibility of another reality (or realities), operating on rules quite different from our own well-known common sense empirical reality, the only one known to most psychologists.'[1] And is the turning to fantasy worlds also a longing for 'another reality'? In a variety of ways many are seeking meaning and direction in secular society today.

2 In the Church

There is also a hunger for spiritual experience and direction amongst Christians. Recent years have seen a boom in the retreat movement, especially directed retreats. Jesuits, with their strong tradition of teaching, now offer updated and biblically based Ignatian retreats with personal direction, and also training in directing others. Monasteries and convents—Catholic, Anglican and Orthodox—welcome many seeking help in spirituality and prayer, as do communities like Taizé and the Community of Celebration. The shepherding within the house church movement has also met a need in people seeking direction, howbeit often given in an over-paternalized way. Courses on prayer get quickly booked up. Nor is the search for direction narrowly pietistic. Many young people are asking hard questions about spirituality and global issues, spirituality and sex, spirituality and war—and Christian spokesmen such as Thomas Merton, Kenneth Leech, Richard Rohr, have encouraged such links. A spirituality not earthed is not biblical.

Although we shall be looking at 'spiritual direction' in its narrower Christian connotation, we need to see it is also relevant to the wider contemporary scene where people are seeking both spirituality and direction.

What Is Spiritual Direction? 3

'Direction' implies making a journey, movement, finding the way, directed living.

And directed rather than aimless living is at the heart of Christian discipleship. We are, as pilgrims, to pursue and live out the values and priorities of the kingdom of God. How? Certainly by walking in the steps of Jesus who is the Way and through the leadings of the Holy Spirit who indwells God's people. The Spirit is the director *par excellence*. Yet such direction rarely happens in a vacuum. We were created for relationship and most of our learning happens in a context of relationship, whether through talking, questioning, discussing, telling, off-loading, or through listening, watching, considering, receiving, taking in. Relationship is vital to personal learning. Many times good teaching in churches is wasted because its hearers never engage with it in a context of personal relationship, whether a one-to-one or a group relationship. Where there are good housegroups personal learning is more likely, though groups are not conducive places for everyone.

'Spiritual direction' originated in monasticism. Whereas in the early church believers were discipled through the teaching and corporate life of the

Christian community, the third and fourth centuries saw many of the devout withdrawing to the Egyptian and Syrian deserts to pray and give themselves to spiritual warfare. One safeguard to counter the excesses of individualism was to find a spiritual 'abba' or director for guidance and support. The 'Apothegmata' or 'Sayings of the Fathers' remain a witness to the simplicity and depth of much of this guidance. Neither was this simply a feature of desert spirituality. Basil of Caesarea (c330–379), bishop, monk, and social reformer, also directed many to self-renouncing service in the marketplace, for 'God the Creator arranged things so that we need each other' (Longer Rule VII). Thus, through the centuries spiritual direction became a resource for personal formation and teaching, either in a one-to-one relationship or in a group. Men and women of God gifted with spiritual discernment and wisdom found that they were, often in quiet and hidden ways, being sought out to help direct Christians of different traditions.

But how does this ministry apply to today's church? Some church leaders (and lay people) are already doing it regularly — guiding individuals in their praying, Bible reading, daily living — others, already over-busy, might well groan at the thought of the faithful queuing up for individual direction. Others again might welcome the very possibility!

At this point we need to say what spiritual direction is not. A spiritual director is not a problem-solver to whom we run for infallible answers. We are to work out our own salvation and Christian discipleship is not a collecting of recipes from others for instant sanctification. Some temperaments hanker after blueprints — 'if only I could find the right formula I'd triumph.' Discovery there might be, but 'we come to God by love and not by navigation' (Augustine). Nor is a spiritual director a guru to whom we turn to satisfy our needs for dependence, even though we may recognize the hand of God providing this particular person at this particular time.[2] Spiritual direction is not an invitation to prolonged introspection, even though personal reflection will be necessary. Nor is it to do with rarefied ascetical exercises, a 'feet off the ground' spirituality. It is not, as some seem to think, necessarily linked with making confession — this may be included but certainly does not have to be.

Spiritual direction is not the same as pastoral counselling or therapy, though there may well be areas of overlap. Brian Hawker, both a spiritual director and pastoral counsellor, says, 'spiritual direction is dealing with eternal realities, pastoral counselling is dealing with problems in the here and now which are blocking me from looking at eternal realities.' Martin Thornton insists that spiritual direction is not need-orientated — helping those in trouble, counselling the disturbed, solving human problems (the 'ambulance syndrome,' he calls it), but 'the positive development of the man-God relation, which is prayer.'[3] He clarifies the difference by comparing the humanistic pastoral counsellor's attitude to suffering as 'something to be relieved,' with the spiritual director's 'which might at least suggest the counterclaim that it was rather something to be interpreted and creatively redeemed.'[4] Kenneth Leech makes a similar point, 'spiritual guidance is not crisis intervention but a continuous process, the movement to God and in God.'[5]

Even so, there are clear links between psychological and spiritual progress if mature integration is to happen. Self-knowledge is close to knowledge of God. The discerning director will want to learn from counselling insights and skills (disciplined listening, empathy, genuineness, appropriate confrontation) together with an understanding of human personality, its development and needs. But he will not accept them uncritically or become imprisoned within them. Likewise, a Christian pastoral counsellor might well be helping to nurture and direct a person's relationship with God through the recognition and healing of blocked or problem areas. The important thing for the pastor who sometimes directs and sometimes counsels is to know what he is doing and when.

The basic premise of spiritual direction is that in order to grow we need each other. Through reflecting on and articulating aspects of my Christian life and discipleship—my hopes and fears, my successes and failures—with someone who will help me look for the Spirit's direction, my private world becomes shared, I can make more sense of my pilgrimage and continue in it supported.

So Thornton says, 'Spiritual direction is the way forward. It is the positive nurture of man's relationship with God, the creative cultivation of charismata; the gifts and graces that all have received.'[6] And for this ministry 'the director needs, or might need, the total picture…because all aspects of life might impinge on the development of prayer.'[7] Merton describes a spiritual director as,

> …concerned with the whole person, for the spiritual life is not just the life of the mind, or of the affections, or of the 'summit of the soul'—it is the life of the whole person.[8]

Gratton too recognizes that,

> Spiritual direction is not concerned only about the spiritual dimension of the person. It is concerned with the whole person, body, soul and spirit combined…The human has its place too…Spiritual direction that ignores the structures of human emergence and its implied limitations as well as its possibilities will not be helpful to real human beings who are called to respond to God's initiative in a truly human and whole manner.[9]

Spiritual direction then, fully includes our humanity but is far more than personal adjustment or social adaptation. It is about a mutual seeking in which one person (the director), mature and skilled in his or her ministry, is alongside another (the directee) in his or her pilgrimage towards Christian maturity and that integration in which the inner and outer person become united. But if it is to do with relationship it needs witnesses. The following share their comments on what they have gained from direction:

> He helped mostly by just being there. He gave me few specific directions, but I could pour out my hopes and fears and failures and be reassured and restored. Knowing this was a great support. If I wrote, his answer might well be on a postcard, but I knew he understood and cared. (A retired bishop)
>
> Just the knowledge of each other's being there is great even though we are scattered. I know we have the Lord but actual flesh and blood is really good too, and clergy so need not to be alone.
> (A deacon belonging to a cell group)
>
> She gives new insights, new ways of looking at things...she helped me begin to see pain as gift and grace. (A Christian counsellor)
>
> A chance for the clergy wife to share in her own right.
> (A curate's wife)

In his *Genesee Diary*, Henri Nouwen wrote of his first encounter with John Eudes, head of the Trappist Abbey of Gethsemani, who was to become his director:

> He gave me much time and attention but did not allow me to waste a minute; he left me fully free to express my feelings and thoughts but did not hesitate to present his own; he offered me space to deliberate about choices and to make decisions but did not withhold his opinion that some choices and decisions were better than others; he let me find my own way but did not hide the map that showed the right direction. In our conversation, John Eudes emerged not only as a listener but also as a guide, not only as a counsellor but also as a director. It did not take me long to realize that this was the man I had needed so badly.[10]

The title 'spiritual director' inevitably smacks of something authoritarian and paternalistic and might deter some from seeking such a relationship. Leech's use of 'soul friend' sounds gentler. Others would prefer 'companion.'

Essentially, though, we are talking about a man or woman of experience, knowledge, and skills; one who sits alongside, rather than above, another. For in spiritual direction the locus of control is in God rather than man. This is the very reason why good spiritual directors do not mind the title because they, more than anyone, recognize that the prime director is the Holy Spirit.

Direction and the Bible 4

In Scripture there are certain recurring themes which support the concept of spiritual direction and to these we now turn.

1 Journey

The story of God's people is one of journeying. As pilgrims the children of Israel journeyed, led by the guiding hand of God. 'Leave your country, your people and your father's household and go to the land I will show you' (Gen 12.1). So Abram set out on a journey where faith rather than sight would be the guiding light, seeking a home, a city, a country. Through desert and warfare, grumblings and fightings, God continued to lead them. Kings led them into battle for the land (eg 2 Kings 8) and prophets pointed them to a righteousness that would bring them to a new highway, a land where mountains would be levelled, rough places smoothed (Is 40.4), and the Prince of Peace would establish his kingdom (Is 9.6).

Jesus taught that discipleship was a journey and following him a narrow path (Mk 8.34). Hebrews describes Christians as 'strangers and nomads' (Heb 11.13 *JB*), Peter calls them 'pilgrims' (1 Pet 2.11 *JB*), and John's Revelation gives glimpses of the final destination, a heavenly city with ever-open gates and a clear flowing stream lined by fruitful trees (Rev 22.1,2). No wonder the theme of journey and pilgrimage has inspired Christian writers ever since:

> With the drawing of this Love and the voice of this Calling we shall not cease from exploration.[11]

And spiritual direction is essentially about a journey where God is guide, Jesus the Way and the Spirit the teacher. As we journey we make our own story which, like the story of God's people, includes creation, pilgrimage, wilderness, promise, deliverance, passion, death and resurrection. Personal reflection helps me discover my whereabouts and articulating this with another encourages me on.

2 Together Not Alone

If we need each other in order to grow then the Christian pilgrimage is not about footing it alone. Of course we shall sometimes feel lonely but we were never meant, grim-faced and tight-lipped, to slog on alone. Mutuality is at the heart of the Godhead, 'the divine litany, the Father to Son to Spirit communication that is going on in the life of God himself.'[12] Rublev's 15th century icon of the Trinity shows three angels seated around a table on which is a chalice. The basic form of composition is a circle, symbol of unity, embracing all three angels. They look at each other in mutual love and self-giving, a trinity yet together revealing the unity of the Godhead.

In both Testaments we see men of God discipling others—Moses and Joshua, Elijah and Elisha, Eli and Samuel, Paul and Timothy. Supremely we see it in Jesus' ministry as he came alongside others. Conversation with Zaccheus led to a radical change of heart and consequently of direction (Lk 19.8,9). With the Samaritan woman he directed discerning answers to her questions and discerning questions to her statements. Again there was a radical change of heart and direction (John 4.1–26). Particularly he spent time directing a group, his twelve disciples, living, eating, travelling with them and teaching about prayer (Lk 11.1–13 and 18.9–14), about worry (Lk 12.22–31), about watchfulness (Lk 12.35–48), about true greatness (Lk 9.46–50). Much of Paul's ministry was spent in directing individuals and groups. Timothy was his 'true son in the faith' (1 Tim 1.2) whom he instructs (1 Tim 1.18 and 4.6). He is to 'set an example' (1 Tim 4.12) to be 'diligent and persevere' (1 Tim 4.15). As a son he is to learn from his father (2 Tim 2.1,2). And Paul did the same for the churches he founded, handing down the Christian tradition not impersonally but as inherited truth within the context of relationship. Letter writing has often been an effective means of direction and Paul made the most of it.

Some Christians know such mutuality in fellowships and house groups. Spiritual direction is not an elite alternative, for a guiding relationship is no substitute either for corporate life and learning within the body of Christ or for everyday relationships. Yet there will also be times when we sit down with someone we trust to open our lives and share our pilgrimage:

> Therefore, a Christian needs another Christian who speaks God's word to him. He needs him again and again when he becomes uncertain and discouraged, for by himself he cannot help himself without belying the truth. He needs his brother man as a bearer and proclaimer of the divine word of salvation.[13]

Another aspect of mutuality is that of spiritual gifts given for mutual upbuilding. Encouragement or exhortation (*paraklesis* (Rom 12.8)) was often used by Paul. Discernment (*diakrisis* 1 Cor 12.10) has always been a key element in spiritual direction, especially in the understanding of spiritual warfare. 'Discernment involves clarity of vision…discerning, discriminating, judging between truth and falsehood.'[14] Gifts of wisdom and knowledge (1 Cor 12.8) are also listed and are important to direction. Pause for a moment and think of someone (or more than one) whom God has used for your own teaching, encouragement, guidance, perhaps in your youth or young adulthood or marriage, or at a crisis point in your life, or very recently. It may have brought much comfort (or much discomfort!), it may have been continuing or a once only meeting but nevertheless was important in that another Christian was alongside to listen and share in such a way that you travelled on encouraged. This is something of what spiritual direction is about.

3 Changing Direction

Jesus taught a way and called himself 'the Way' (Jn 14.6). The challenge of his person and teaching involves a turnabout, a change of direction involving heart and action, repentance (*metanoia*). And this is not a once only experience but a continuing one. We cannot do it for ourselves, it is gift and grace—God acting on and in us to create a new willingness to see with his eyes, think with his mind, adopt his values and attitudes (1 Cor 2.16; Phil 2.5). *Metanoia* is about transformation and God is agent and goal (2 Cor 3.18: NB the passive mood *'metamorphoumetha'*). 'It is grace that transforms and not human effort, and that applies to every aspect of the Christian life from the beginning to the very end.'[15] But our 'yes' is necessary, the 'yes' of faith which is 'the empty hand that we hold out to Christ and that he fills with himself, and the impulse and strength to stretch out the hand comes from the Spirit.'[16] 'Yes' is for each day as God seeks to implement in us changes of thinking, choosing, and feeling. Spiritual direction makes opportunity for self-examination 'in order to uncover the sins, failures and inconsistencies which contradict the following of Christ and the love of God and neighbour.'[17] If self-examination is not to deteriorate into introspection or be ignored we need wise guides with whom to articulate the inner movement of our spirits and the outer movement of our lives.

4 Progress

If the grace of God is all gift, there is also consequent human effort needed and Paul uses some strenuous metaphors for this. The Christian is like an athlete in training (1 Cor 9.24–27). *Askeo* means to train, exercise, endeavour (thus *askesis*, 'ascetical'), and Paul exhorts Corinthian Christians to 'run in such a way as to get the prize' (1 Cor 9.24; *NEB* 'Run to win'). He himself 'presses on (strains forward) to take hold of that for which Jesus Christ took hold of me' (Phil 3.13). Coaching involves knowledge which can be either taught or practically applied and Thornton looks helpfully at the role of the director as spiritual coach:

> The coach is not necessarily the better player…It is satisfying to play a game well but there can be greater satisfaction in coaching another to higher standards…One of the supreme blessings for the spiritual director is to watch his client surpass him…which frequently happens.[18]

Paul also uses battle language. The Christian is a soldier in training needing to learn how to get equipped for battle (*askeo* can also have a military connotation: see 2 Tim 2.3 and Eph 6.10–17). Another concept Paul uses that speaks of progress is growth into maturity (Eph 4.14–15). We are to 'put off' the old self and 'put on' the new (Eph 4.22–24), which will involve moral, mental, emotional, and behavioural, changes. And moral change is also part of his metaphor of fruitfulness—a picture of growth and progress (Gal 5.22–23).

These pictures speak of the kind of movement that implies progress and therefore appeal to us. But what about movement that feels backwards rather than forwards, down rather than up? Metaphors of growth must be used with care and 'which way is forwards?' can be a right question to ask. Bewildering reversals will sometimes be part of the journey:

> In order to arrive at what you are not
> You must go through the way in which you are not.[19]

Darkness can be necessary to progress, whether it be the cloud hiding the sun (as, for example, in Ex 13.21), or the earth covering the seed (Jn 12.24), or the deep pit without foothold (Ps 88.4).

Chaos may sometimes be an important condition of growth, the chaos leading to new integration. Pruning precedes fruitfulness (Jn 15.2), dryness can increase our longing for water[20] and emptiness our capacity for God. Comforts and consolations may appear to wean us from the gifts to the Giver. Staretz Sophrony, an Orthodox priest, said:

> In following Christ's commands a person will feel less and less capable. 'Progress' is to do with death itself, an increasingly profound death.

Lest we settle for limited models of productivity, we must see the cross as the ruling principle of the Christian life, for there can be no true reflection of Christ that does not consist of bearing his cross. It is through suffering that we learn obedience and trust, and God, in his wisdom, will lead us through stages of growth that feel like anything but growth to bring us to Christlikeness.

> A condition of complete simplicity (costing not less than everything).[21]

It is in the darkest, unprogressive times that I return to base and say '*baptizatus sum*,' 'I am a baptized person'—and that is sheer gift and grace.

Spiritual Direction in the History of the Church

5

From a wealth of historical material we shall briefly look at examples illustrating three working models.

1 One-to-one Direction

Many towns in the Middle Ages sought to have as part of their local welfare services a Christian recluse whose chief work was prayer and availability to people as spiritual adviser. Julian of Norwich (1342–1420) was much sought after for her wisdom. She regarded herself as a woman, 'unlettered, feeble and frail' yet comes across with sanity, strength and tenderness. After receiving a series of visions she wrote down her *Revelations of Divine Love* and, 20 years later, a longer version including meditative material. Her intention in writing was chiefly pastoral. Captivated by Christ and his love she 'was greatly moved with love for my fellow Christians that they might know and see what I was seeing, for I wanted to cheer them too.' She describes Christ's dying love on the cross in graphic detail, teaches about love's triumph over sin, and gives practical advice about prayer. The images she uses—the hazelnut, the herring scales, the seabed, the clothes blown in the wind—show how she reflected on life in East Anglia and on God at work in his world. One can imagine how ordinary people coming to her for help would have gone away cheered and instructed by this sane visionary.

Many towns in the Middle Ages sought to have a Christian recluse whose chief work was prayer and availability as spiritual adviser

Our Lord says, 'pray inwardly, even if you do not enjoy it. It does good, though you feel nothing, see nothing, yes, even though you are doing nothing. For when you are dry, empty, sick, or weak, at such a time is your prayer most pleasing to me though you find little enough to enjoy in it.'[22]

Flee to the Lord and we shall be strengthened. Touch him, and we shall be cleansed. Cling to him, and we shall be safe and sound from every danger. For it is the will of our courteous Lord that we should be as much at home with him as heart may think or soul desire.[23]

2 Direction Through Letters

Personal correspondence has been a significant means of direction down the years. Probably many of us have treasured letters containing gems of spiritual guidance which have come to us when the writer could not, or during times of personal need or crisis. The length of that sort of letter hardly matters—one sentence might give six months' nourishment, or a paragraph may become food for reflection.

One sentence might give six months' nourishment, or a paragraph may become food for reflection

Samuel Rutherford (c1600–1661) during nine years of pastoral ministry in the small parish of Anwoth, Galloway, believed passionately that the gospel of Christ should shape the character and life of his people and the 'cure of souls' was central to his spirituality and ministry. His letters, published within three years of his death, were widely read in Scottish homes. To Marion McKnaught, whose husband appears to have been falsely accused in the local town council, he wrote,

> Sister, remember how many thousands of talents of sins your Master hath forgiven you: forgive ye therefore your fellow-servants one talent...Be not cast down: if ye saw Him, who is standing on the shore holding out His arms to welcome you to land, you would not only wade through a sea of wrongs, but through hell itself, to be at Him.[24]

C S Lewis would probably have laughed at being called a spiritual director, yet many of his letters contain such insights. In reply to a letter from Sheldon Vanauken, who, after his wife's death, wrote to Lewis about their love which had remained for him an end in itself, Lewis replied:

> One way or another the thing had to die. Perpetual springtime is not allowed. You are not cutting the wood of life according to the grain...You have been treated with a severe mercy. You have been brought to see (how true and very frequent this is!) that you were jealous of God. So from US you have been led back to US AND GOD; it remains to go on to GOD AND US.

Vanauken comments,

> After this severe and splendid letter I loved Lewis like a brother. A brother and father combined.[25]

3 Direction in Groups

Spiritual direction need not be limited to a twosome. Church history offers many examples of how it can happen in a group context. Richard Baxter (1615–1691) during 14 years of pastoral ministry at Kidderminster gave himself to the pastoral care of some 800 families. He was concerned that preachers of the Word should also take it into homes and minister it at closer quarters. He set aside every Monday and Tuesday for personal ministry of the Scriptures to whole families, listening to them, pastoring them, and teaching them. The Clapham circle, functioning at the turn of the 18th and 19th centuries, was a means of mutual direction for Charles Simeon, William Wilberforce, and others.

Church history offers many examples of how it can happen in a group context

The early days of Methodism saw a similar concern for group direction. From 1742 Methodist societies were organized into 'classes' of 8–10 persons, each with a leader, based on Wesley's conviction that spiritual oversight needed to be intimate and personal. He wrote:

> It can scarce be conceived what advantages have been reaped from this little prudential regulation. Many now happily experienced that Christian fellowship of which they had not so much as an idea before. They began to 'bear one another's burdens,' and naturally to 'care for each other.' As they had daily a more intimate acquaintance with, so they had a more endeared affection for, each other. And 'speaking the truth in love, they grew up into Him, in all things, who is the Head, even Christ.'[26]

Leaders 'found their highest joy in the cure of souls committed to them'

The duties of class leaders (women as well as men in 1847) were to 'ask each member in turn to speak of their experience in the Christian life, after which he (she) would give a word of encouragement, advice or reproof, as was necessary.'[27] No wonder leaders 'found their highest joy in the cure of souls committed to them, and they accepted the responsibility of their office as a most sacred trust.'[28]

So far we have sought to define spiritual direction, provide some biblical undergirding, and give some examples. In this second part we shall look at what is required of a spiritual director and suggest some ways of exploring it as a personal resource.

6

What Sort of Person?

Good directors are neither numerous nor ready-made.

Their ministry tends to be a background rather than a foreground one. There are probably more of them quietly getting on with it than is apparent, though they may not call themselves 'spiritual directors'—clergy, religious, lay people, tutors in jobs where Christian formation is important. They should not be self-appointed. What then should they be? Someone who finds people turning to him (or her) for spiritual counsel or direction might start by considering the importance of four kinds of knowledge—of God, of the tools of his trade, of others, and of himself.

1 Knowing God

If I am attempting to guide others in their pilgrimage I too must be a traveller, perhaps further on but still travelling, seeking, discovering. If the journey to God is the agenda of our meeting, then I too will be continuing to pray, meditate, think, and have both a prayer discipline and a living theology of prayer. I shall be open to the prayer of listening to God.[29] 'In prayer we are gradually hollowed out to become more *"capax Dei"'* (capacity for God), said Maria Boulding, and someone pastoring others will be only too aware of the need to receive even at the price of felt (and often uncomfortable) emptiness. Father Sophrony says of his ministry as spiritual director, 'the way is to pray every day with a flaming heart "Do not permit me to be wrong in my work for this service transcends my capacity." It is not *human* capacity that will do it. "Without me you can do nothing!"'

> *If I am attempting to guide others in their pilgrimage I too must be a traveller*

The director will also pray for the gifts necessary for his ministry—discernment (1 Cor 12.10; see Luke 7.39–47, Jn 4.1–26, Acts 5.1–11), which listens with compassion and truth through the layers of a person; encouragement (Rom 12.8), to help people on their way; wisdom (1 Cor 12.8), often given when the director is least aware of it. Barsanuphius, a sixth century director, wrote:

> I said nothing from myself, but I prayed, and then said whatever God gave me the confidence to say...when the need arose, God opened even the ass's mouth.[30]

Michael Ramsey says more pithily, 'Rely on your consecrated hunch!'

Those guiding others should themselves be being guided for 'he who is a spiritual director to himself is counsellor to a fool' (Bernard). It is all too easy for Christian leaders to become increasingly cut off. If they are to guide others they too must know the resource of guidance.

Think of some who have influenced you through their knowledge of God. Sanctity has little to do with a pietistic other-worldliness and much to do with ordinariness and simplicity—being oneself in God, accepted by the Father, met by the Son, and indwelt by the living Spirit.

2 Knowing the Tools of the Trade

St Teresa put learning as a high priority in spiritual guides. But what kind of learning? A director needs to know and use the tools of his trade. Firstly, he needs to know the Bible. Clement of Alexandria said that the true seeker after God would be 'in and out of the Scriptures every day.' Someone directing others needs to know the Bible as his own resource of study and meditation, to know its teaching about man's relationship with God in covenant, encounter, incorporation, to know both its teaching on prayer and those who in its pages are seen at prayer. Secondly, he needs an ever-deepening understanding of Christian doctrine. To see why someone relates more to the transcendent Father, or to the incarnate Son,

A director needs knowledge and experience of different sorts of prayer

or to the indwelling Spirit, he needs a growing understanding of the Trinity. To help someone develop his individual gifts he needs an understanding of the complementarity of the individual and the corporate within the church, the Body of Christ. To help someone see the nature of his justification (and live by it) he needs an ever-deepening understanding of grace. Thirdly, he needs knowledge and experience of different sorts of prayer and those in history who have explored them. If someone is finding words burdensome he may need an introduction to the prayer of quiet or the Jesus Prayer.[31] If he needs to use his body in prayer, encourage him to.[32] If he wants greater unity between work and prayer, introduce him to Brother Lawrence.[33] If he needs a more imaginative approach to biblical meditation, show him the Ignatian method.[34] For some, a new way of praying will be a welcome release from the straitjacket of past patterns.[35]

3 Knowing Another

Essentially a director must believe in the person he is guiding. It was said of the Curé D'Ars that he believed in those who came to him more than they believed in themselves. One feels vulnerable in baring one's soul to another, so respect, compassion, and commitment, are essential. So too is disciplined listening, and those guiding others should learn some of the skills of pastoral counselling.[36] The director will discover what is significant in the other person's life. A Russian director, criticized for spending time advising an old peasant woman about the care of her turkeys, replied, 'Not at all, her whole life is in those turkeys.'[37]

Appropriate confrontation is also necessary. The director needs freedom to offer it and the other person freedom to receive it, and this very much depends on the trustful quality of the relationship already built. Spiritual direction is not simply a cosy chat, and being straight with a person may be one of the most important contributions you make. After one such painful confrontation someone wrote, 'Thank you for being straight with me—I needed it.' Likewise we shall sometimes need to challenge a person's values—there are sins before God which are not necessarily sins before society. Our concern to hold him into God's truth will be greater than our concern for him to become adjusted to society.

The director needs freedom to offer confrontation and the other person freedom to receive it

Very clearly we are not in the business of directing people into modes of prayer that are unsuitable for them. It is all too easy to do this, especially if we know no other ways of praying than our own. To encourage the basically extrovert person to develop his praying in a way more suited to the introvert is to do him a disservice, and since many books on prayer are written by introverts we can quickly fall into this trap. The world-affirming person should not be forced into a world-renouncing spirituality, nor someone who is essentially a thinker into an affective spirituality. Basically a person's own spiritual propensity is to be encouraged whether similar to or different from one's own.[38]

4 Knowing Oneself

A spiritual director's own life experience is one of his greatest assets. He knows he has not arrived—he is still travelling—but he has learnt through the experiences of life and there is a maturity about him.

What will characterize growing maturity? An integration of my own life-experience through reflection, self-examination and help from others. 'A guide who has not encountered his own passions, his own inner conflicts, who does not truly know his darkness and his light, will be of no value in the spiritual battle.'[39] As his life-experience, including suffering, becomes integrated so he can put it at the disposal of others, explicitly and implicitly. It is only as we become at ease with the condition of our own humanity that we can accept another person's. This will give birth to humility in us, and humility will help us resist the temptation to play God to people.

Maturing through self-knowledge will lead us truly to put self aside for the sake of another

Maturing through self-knowledge will lead us truly to put self aside for the sake of another. Particularly this will show itself in the gift of availability to another, a conducive meeting-place, the courtesy of taking the phone off the hook, keeping confidences and having grace to forget as well as remember things people tell us. We shall not feel obliged to fill silences with words but learn to speak out of silence. Someone told me how her director always says at the end of her outpourings, 'Let us keep silent and wait on the Holy Spirit.' And they do for 5–10 minutes, then he speaks out of the silence, 'and I know what he is saying is of the Holy Spirit—it resonates so clearly in me and rings true.'

Self-knowledge yes—but humour too. Richard Rolle wrote in the 14th century of spiritual direction as 'full merry counsel with his ghostly Father.' It would be a pity if our spirituality did not increase in us the ability sometimes to laugh, especially at ourselves!

7 Patterns for Today

1 Reflection

Before looking at one-to-one and group direction it is worth thinking about the place and content of reflection in our lives. Socrates said that the unexamined life is not worth living. If life is nothing more than a moving from one activity to the next it is not surprising if we become restless, cluttered and superficial. 'Superficiality is the curse of our age…The desperate need today is…for deep people.'[40] Depth is acquired partly by learning to be reflective, taking time to reflect on the world around us and how we spend our lives. Its end is not introspection which, taken to extremes, can become an opting out of life, but integration, a gathering up of the fragments to find, under the hand of God, a wholeness in living.

One way to begin is to keep a daily journal. It can be either a simple or much fuller one. Whether shorter or longer, the important thing is to make it serve you so that it becomes not a burden but a means of personal reflection and integration. A simple way is to use a notebook, dating each day and following these headings:

a   insights, thoughts, questions emerging from my Bible reading and prayer;
b   notes about my spiritual journey—things that are currently concerning me, challenging me, strengthening me;
c   something I am reading or thinking about at present that I would like to remember;
d   a current event or relationship I need to reflect on.

For a fuller version the following headings might be useful:

a   my personal salvation history (it can be both encouraging and revealing to review one's life journey and trace the different stages within it. Each of us has a Bethlehem, a wilderness, a Good Friday, an Easter Sunday, a Pentecost, though they do not necessarily occur chronologically or once only);
b   my vocation—the work, ministry, roles I am called to and the gifts I have been given for these;

c   my ongoing journey and significant events in it;
d   my path in prayer;
e   the place of the Bible in my life;
f   other kinds of reading and study and their influence on me;
g   things that cause me blocking, bondage, fear, sin, shortcoming (where I will sometimes need another's help especially if they involve my past. 'There is no healing of the memory until the memory itself is exposed…the word of forgiveness is not audible for the one who has not "turned" to his or her past'[41]);
h   lifestyle;
i   recreation (ie re-creation!);
j   relationships in my life (family, friends, work colleagues, neighbours);
k   my place within the people of God (in my church, house group);
l   use of money and giving.
m   solitude and retreat.

The idea is not to attempt all these at once—rather they could be used as sections in a loose leaf file and added to at intervals. It is helpful to date entries. Out of this material will emerge some of the items you may want to discuss with a spiritual director.[42]

Some find it helpful to reflect last thing at night as a prayerful self-examination, for example:

a   Ask for God's light on the past day. This is not your own analysis but what the Holy Spirit wants to show you.
b   Review the day and see where you need to give thanks. (It will not necessarily be through feeling thankful.) Express your gratitude to God.
c   Ask God to show you how he has been present in your life today, in you and others. How have you responded to his leadings? Think of your moods and see what stands out—joy, pain, turmoil, love, anger, anxiety, the presence of God, isolation etc. Is there any one area you are being asked to focus on for prayer or action?
d   Confess to God those times when you have sinned and tell him you are sorry for going your own way.
e   Commit yourself to God for the night.

2 One-to-one Direction

By now some may well be asking 'Where can I look for a spiritual director? And if I find someone what shall I say?'

Spiritual direction may well develop within a context of friendship. There are both advantages and disadvantages to this. To be already known and understood gives an obvious head-start but since this is a particular sort of meeting, disciplined boundaries and clear objectives need to be set by both parties. One might prefer a priest or minister and sometimes retired clergy have both the experience and time for this sort of ministry. But lay people can also make good directors—perhaps someone you have known for years, or, say, your house group leader. Or you may have to seek one out. Some dioceses are now running training courses in spiritual direction and a Diocesan Education Officer might know someone suitable. If you have a monastery or convent nearby it is worth enquiring there too, for those who have spent years in a ministry of prayer can have much to offer. If there is no-one nearby it is well worth time and money to travel to a good director, perhaps with visits twice or three times a year. Another possibility is to attend an individually conducted retreat. An increasing number of monasteries and convents offer an eight days' Ignatian retreat where the focus is on personal Bible meditation. Each day the retreatant has a few suggested passages given by his director who meets him once a day for sharing and reflection. Above all, if you need someone, pray. You will eventually be shown where to turn. It may turn out to be one or two meetings only or a much longer period of time. (Richard Foster used Dallas Willard as his director for over four years and reckons his life to be 'the embodiment' of the teaching in *Celebration of Discipline*).

The kind of person you are looking for is indicated in chapter 6 but other questions to ask yourself might be:

- is this someone I can respect?

- is this someone with whom I can be really honest?

- is this someone with whom I can learn?

In making initial contact with someone, write or speak to him (or her) about what you are looking for—someone with whom to discuss your Christian life and pilgrimage. If he is not used to the concept you may need to do some initial explaining, but, once he understands your expectation, he may turn out far better than he imagined!

It is important to attend your first meeting prepared:

- be prepared to talk about yourself, including information that will show him your background, present life circumstances, and your Christian pilgrimage. Think this through beforehand.

- be prepared to share with him your present pattern of prayer and how this relates to patterns of corporate worship in your own church. You have nothing to lose and everything to gain by being completely honest, even if you feel your devotional life is in a mess. That is one reason why you are seeking help.

- be prepared to tell him any particular things he should know (eg you spend a long time travelling to and from work each day; you have recently had a bereavement in your family; you have to get up each night for the children).

- be prepared to open up any particular areas where you are seeking guidance, or new learning, or particular goals (see previous section on reflection).

You may need help over self-discipline, praying for others, using the gift of tongues, suitable reading, dryness, finding your praying is very different from others in your house group. Direction is not simply for times of crisis but for ongoing growth.

Some of the items on my own agenda for spiritual direction over the past two or three years have been: lifestyle—being overbusy and needing to rediscover a rhythm where prayer finds its right place alongside a full teaching and pastoral ministry; bereavement and particular aspects of my mother's death; reading; pain in prayer; spiritual warfare; a major decision. Some of the learning and insights gained come back to me with great clarity as I write. Our sessions together (usually about one hour each) included talking, listening, crying, laughing, praying, and I continue to be thankful for the encouragement, challenge, prayer, assurance of forgiveness and support which they provided.

Would there ever be reason to stop such a relationship? Sometimes. If you feel the 'fit' is wrong so that the relationship is not working well you might need to consider ending it, for there should be a growing sense of ease as you get to know each other. Occasionally a director gives bad direction. We are clearly never obliged to follow any human direction contrary to what we know to be scriptural or morally right. On the other hand, running to a succession of people for direction may well indicate our own immaturity and instability. We rarely find one who provides answers to all our questions, meets all our expectations and generally measures up to perfection! Moreover the relationship is never an end in itself. A director is only 'God's usher' to lead us to our real Director. For this reason alone he needs our prayers as he seeks, all too aware of his own fallibility, to fulfil his ministry responsibly.

3 Group Direction

Aware as we are these days of groups and their many uses, little exploration has been made until recently of the group as a context for spiritual direction. In this final section we look at some examples.

Previously we considered one person as director and and one as directed, but direction can also be mutual, each in turn directing the other. In his *Life Together* Bonhoeffer told how he tried this in his experimental community before World War II. Based on the teaching of Jesus about confessing faults one to the other, each brother chose another and they confessed to and directed each other. This kind of mutuality can certainly happen between friends, though there must be a clear understanding by each as to the nature of the exercise, a proper respect for confidences and for each other's judgment.

The cell group of three or more people who pray together and discuss their growth and life in God also has its place. This happens in the Kimbanguist Church in Zaire where they have small cells for mutual confession. This has also been a feature of the East African revival and was probably also present in Watchman Nee's church. In this country there has been some experimenting with different sorts of cell groups.

Some clergy belong to 'Jesus Caritas' groups. At each meeting one person lays before the others some current situation where he is in need of guidance and wisdom. After he has spoken the group members wait in silence, praying, listening to God, open to receive. Then they speak out of the silence bringing their insights to the person.

Interest was awakened for some when a TV programme about Archbishop Robert Runcie showed him with his cell group. A few weeks later, whilst visiting St John's College, he shared with us about the mutual support within the group and the high priority given to it by its members. Some of our final year students who were soon to be ordained, feeling the need for some kind of support system, especially during the first few years of ministry, decided to create their own cells. There are now several in existence, some of which I have monitored and note, with their permission, certain findings.

Cell A comprises a group of six (men and women, married and single) all in full-time church ministry. They chose each other carefully before leaving college on the basis of previously existing friendship. They decided to meet for 24 hours every nine months with an initial commitment of three years. So far they have had four cell meetings with time to share their situations, discuss, pray, and relax, together. If anyone wants specific spiritual direction they seek to give it. They also pray for each other at a distance and give each other freedom to phone at any hour of the day or night if necessary for personal support. (One has taken advantage of a night call). So far they list the advantages of the group as: getting away together, mutual support, time to reflect, being straight with each other, mutual prayer.

Cell B comprises a group of seven (three married clergy couples and one single woman deacon). They also chose each other before leaving college on the basis of friendship. They meet for 48 hours every eight months and have a rotating leadership for group sessions. Some of their agreed objectives are:

- to provide an opportunity for each member to share the joys and sorrows of the past months, with the opportunity to receive prayer and/or ministry;
- to provide a forum where we can review the content and balance of our lives as far as work, personal spirituality, family time, leisure, outside interests etc go; each of us will be open to the counsel of the rest of the group as to possible areas of change;
- to provide consistent prayer support for each other and our families and to be open to receive prayer requests for each other at any time of the day or night;
- to provide meetings which have about them a sense of mental, spiritual and emotional homecoming to them.

Each person in this cell has personal time allotted to use as he or she wants and this requires preparation and reflection beforehand. So far advantages include: listening to each other, the opportunity to defuse strong feelings, mutual trust. 'We trust and appreciate each other's discernment given by the Lord and recognize his authority in each other. The bond between us enables us to pray into each other's situations—it is different from friends simply getting together' wrote one member of this cell.

Cell C comprises four people (one married couple, and two single deacons). Their mutual commitment is strong and their sharing deep. 'We have "permission" to share and question on a deep and challenging level without fear of losing friends...We are prepared to travel the length of the country to meet...There has to be a willingness among all the members of such a group to be prepared to give and take, to offer criticism and receive it, to encourage and to be encouraged etc.'

Could there be pointers here as to how some clergy and wives could find more resources in mutuality for their heavy ministerial demands?

The Superior of an Anglican convent, writing about the cell she belonged to (which includes members from outside her community), considered the essential factors in such cells were:

- they should meet in a neutral situation.
- they should be a 'peer' group in so far as the relationship within the group is on an equal footing.

- they should come together at regular intervals and meetings should, if possible, be reckoned as sacrosanct engagements.
- meetings should be long enough to provide opportunity for fun and relaxation as well as worship and discussion.

Her cell met every nine months, each giving an account of himself or herself and others responding, commenting, advising, suggesting. She spoke of it as a tremendously rich and enlarging experience, 'Friendship expressed at its very best, I think.'

Is there anything in this for church house groups? David Prior believes there would be real value in a house group seeing the provision of such spiritual direction and help as latent within the group itself. Whilst this is expecting a great deal for such groups, a measure of personal ministry to the individual plus group ministry to one another would seem to preserve the right balance. One church's house groups were doing this as they made a study, chapter by chapter, of Richard Foster's *Celebration of Discipline*. Another house group looks together, from time to time, at personal affairs of group members (eg job interview, family sickness, finance). Many groups have not yet discovered that degree of mutual trust. There are clearly possibilities to explore here so that members of such groups see group guidance as normal rather than exceptional. Obviously there can be abuses of any group: authoritarian leadership, group pressure, loss of individual responsibility. But the possibilities can greatly outweigh such things if groups are well taught, and some of these expressions of mutual direction could well offer ways forward out of the isolated, anxious states of living of these days and into the fellowship of God's people.

We all need someone who will carry us through our nights and days, our winters and summers, and our times of darkness and clarity. We all need someone who knows the secret of our hearts.[43]

Speaking the truth in love, we are to grow up in every way into him who is the Head, into Christ from whom the whole body, joined and knit together by every joint with which it is supplied, when each part is working properly, makes bodily growth and upbuilds itself in love (Eph. 4.15–16).

You may find it helpful, having read this booklet, to ask yourself:

a   What experiences of spiritual direction have I found helpful in my own life?
b   Would some kind of spiritual direction be an enrichment to me currently?
c   If so, how could I go about finding it?

Appendix: Resources

8

1 For Further Reading

Barry and Connolly, *The Practice of Spiritual Direction* (Seabury Press)

Gerard Hughes, *God of Surprises* (DLT)

Kenneth Leech, *Soul Friend* (Sheldon Press, 1977)

Adrian von Kamm, *In Search of Spiritual Identity* (New Jersey: Dimension Books)

Richard Foster, *Celebration of Discipline* (Hodder and Stoughton)

Richard Foster, *Study Guide to Celebration of Discipline* (Hodder and Stoughton)

Carolyn Gratton, *Guidelines for Spiritual Direction* (New Jersey: Dimension Books, 1980)

Margaret Guenther, *Holy Listening* (DLT, 1992)

Gordon Jeff, *Spiritual Direction for Every Christian* (SPCK)

C S Lewis, *Letters to an American Lady* (Hodder and Stoughton, 1967)

Nemeck and Coombs, *The Way of Spiritual Direction* (The Liturgical Press, Minnesota 1985)

Brother Ramon SSF, *Deeper into God* (Marshall Pickering)

Martin Thornton, *Spiritual Direction* (SPCK, 1984)Tilden Edwards, *Spiritual Friend — Reclaiming the Gift of Spiritual Direction* (New York: Paulist Press, 1980)

2 Further Resources

Spi-Dir is an ecumenical network which seeks to promote, support and resource those involved in the ministry of spiritual direction. See their web site at www.oxford.anglican.org/spi-dir/

The Retreat Association publishes the *Retreats* journal, which gives details of Retreat Centres (tel 0845 456 1429). Their web site also has information and free downloadable leaflets covering a range of topics including choosing a spiritual guide (www.retreats.org.uk).

Notes

1 Carl Rogers, *Some New Challenges*, p 385 quoted by Kevin Culligan OCD, *Towards a Contemporary Model of Spiritual Direction: A Comparative Study of St John of the Cross and Carl Rogers*, Carmelite Studies Vol 2 (ICS Public, 1982) p 149.

2 cf Some Eastern models of spiritual direction where the authority of the guru is absolute.

3 Martin Thornton, *Spiritual Direction* (SPCK, 1984) p 10.

4 *ibid*, p 12.

5 Kenneth Leech, *Soul Friend* (Sheldon Press, 1977) p 96.

6 Martin Thornton, *op cit*, p 10.

7 *ibid*, p 29.

8 Thomas Merton, *Spiritual Direction and Meditation* (Anthony Clarke, 1975) p 15.

9 Carolyn Gratton, *Guidelines for Spiritual Direction* (Dimension Books, 1980) p 158.

10 Henri Nouwen, *The Genesee Diary* (Image Books, 1981) p 15.

11 T S Eliot, *Little Gidding*, see also hymns eg 'Guide me, O thou great Redeemer' and John Bunyan's, *Pilgrim's Progress*.

12 T A Smail, *The Forgotten Father* (Hodder and Stoughton, 1980) p 144.

13 D Bonhoeffer, *Life Together* (SCM, 1949) p 12.

14 Kenneth Leech, *op cit*, p 131.

15 T A Smail, *Reflected Glory* (Hodder and Stoughton, 1975) p 28.

16 *ibid*, p 30.

17 Christopher Bryant, *Jung and the Christian Way* (Darton, Longman and Todd, 1983) p 78.

18 M Thornton, *op cit*, p 28.

19 T S Eliot, *East Coker*.

20 See T H Green, *When the Well Runs Dry* (Ave Maria Press, 1979).

21 T S Eliot, *Little Gidding*.

22 Julian of Norwich (Clifton Wolters ed), *Revelations of Divine Love* (Penguin Classics) p 124.

23 *ibid*, p 200.

24 *The Loveliness of Christ* from *The Letters of Samuel Rutherford 1600–1661*, selected by E S Lister (Samuel Bagster, 1958) pp 115–116.

25 Sheldon Vanauken, *A Severe Mercy* (Hodder and Stoughton, 1977) pp 209–210.

26 Thomas Jackson (ed), *The Works of John Wesley* (London: John Mason, 1829–31) Vol VIII, p 253.

27 R C Swift, *Lively People* (Dept of Adult Education, University of Nottingham, 1982) p 142.

28 Thomas Jackson (ed), *op cit*, p 253.

29 See Michael Mitton, *The Wisdom to Listen* (Grove Pastoral booklet P 5).

30 Source unknown.

31 See Simon Barrington-Ward and Brother Ramon, *Praying the Jesus Prayer Together* (Bible Reading Fellowship, 2001) and Keith Hubbard, *In the Name of Jesus* (Grove Spirituality booklet S 72)

32 *ibid*, ch 4.

33 Brother Lawrence, *The Practice of the Presence of God* (Epworth, 1959).

34 For example, Richard Foster, *Celebration of Discipline*, pp 22–3 and p 26.

35 For a thorough and helpful study of these 'tools,' see M Thornton, *Spiritual Direction* (SPCK, 1984). See too Richard Foster, *Celebration of Discipline*.

36 This might well apply to other aspects of personality development and needs such as projection and transference, distinguishing between a 'dark night' and a clinical depression, being aware of when help other than, or as well as, ours is needed.

37 Thomas Merton, *Spiritual Direction* (Anthony Clarke, 1975) p 16.

38 Ruth Fowke, *Personality and Prayer* (Eagle).

39 Kenneth Leech, *op cit*, p 89.

40 Richard Foster, *op cit*, p 1.

41 Rowan Williams, *Resurrection* (Darton, Longman and Todd, 1982) p 21.

42 Harold Miller, *Finding a Personal Rule of Life* (Grove Spirituality booklet S 8).

43 Jean Vanier, *Community and Growth* (Darton, Longman and Todd, 1979) p 178.